Life Can
Be Hard
Sometimes

...but It's Going
to Be Okay

A collection of poems
Edited by Susan Polis Schutz

Library of Congress Catalog Card Number: 90-80731
ISBN: 0-88396-281-0

ACKNOWLEDGMENTS appear on page 62.

design on book cover is registered in
U.S. Patent and Trademark Office.

Manufactured in the United States of America
First Printing: March, 1990

Blue Mountain Press ®

P.O. Box 4549, Boulder, Colorado 80306

CONTENTS

It's Going to Be Okay...
Just Hang in There

It's going to be okay.

Just give things a little time.
And in the meantime...
  keep believing in yourself;
  take the best of care;
  try to put things in perspective;
  remember what's most important;
  don't forget that someone cares;
  search for the positive side;
  learn the lessons to be learned;
  and find your way through to the
  inner qualities:
    the strength, the smiles,
    the wisdom, and the
    optimistic outlook
  that are such special parts
    of you.

It's going to be okay.

—Barin Taylor

When Life Isn't Easy,
May You Remember This . . .

May you know, in your heart, that
 others are always thinking of you.
May you always have rainbows that
 follow the rain.
May you celebrate the wonderful things
 about you.
And when tomorrow comes, may you
 do it all over again.

May you remember how full of smiles
 the days can be.
May you believe that what you search for,
 you will see.
May you find time to smell the flowers,
 and find time to share
  the beauty of you.

May you envision today as a gift,
   and tomorrow as another.
May you add a meaningful page to the
   diary of each new day,
   and may you make
   "living happily ever after. . ."
something that will really come true.

And may you always keep planting
   the seeds of your dreams.
      Because if you keep
         believing in them,
   they'll keep trying their best . . .
         to blossom for you.

—Collin McCarty

If Ever You Need Me,
I Hope You'll Let Me Know

No one ever said life would be easy,
and it seems so unfair sometimes.
Yet life's ups and downs
make us better and stronger,
even though we may not realize it
   at the moment.

Remember —
when you hurt, let the pain out.
When you're sad, let the tears flow.
When you're angry, release it.
When frustration sets in, work it out.

Help yourself as much as you can.
You can be your own best friend.

But when you need to share
your confusion, let me know.
I try to know when to be there,
but I can't always
unless you let me know.

Love is the greatest gift
we can give to one another,
and giving is one of the
greatest joys life bestows upon us.

I'm here to give to you,
whenever and for always.

—Laurie Wymer

From Every Change in Life,
You Can Learn Something Important

In every change
that you experience in life,
there will be times when
you'll wonder if you can endure.
But you'll learn that facing
each difficulty one by one
isn't so hard.
It's when you don't deal
with a situation
that it sometimes comes back
to confront you again.

Changes are sometimes very painful,
but they teach us
that we can endure
and that we can become stronger.
Everything that comes into your life
has a purpose,
but the outcome is in your hands
by the action you take.
Be wise with your life,
be willing to endure,
and always be willing
to face life's challenges.

—Sherrie L. Householder

You Have the Power
to Make Your Life Everything
You Want It to Be

This life is yours
Take the power
to choose what you want to do
and do it well
Take the power
to love what you want in life
and love it honestly
Take the power
to walk in the forest
and be a part of nature
Take the power
to control your own life
No one else can do it for you
Nothing is too good for you
You deserve the best
Take the power
to make your life
healthy
exciting
worthwhile
and very happy

—Susan Polis Schutz

Just Do Your Best,
and Everything Will Be All Right

It's not always easy to know
which path to follow, which
decision to make, or what to do.

Life is a series of new horizons,
new hopes, new days, and changes
that come to you. And we all need
some help with these things from time to time.

Remember these things: Dream it. Do it. And
discover how special you are. Be positive,
for your attitude will affect the outcome of
many things. Ask for help when you need it;
seek the wisdom the world holds and hold on
to it. Make some progress every single day.
Begin. Believe. And become.

Give yourself all the credit you're due; don't
shortchange your qualities, your abilities, or
any of the things that are so unique about you.
Remember how precious life can be. Imagine.
Invest the time it takes to reach out for your
dreams; it will bring you happiness that no
money on earth can buy. Don't be afraid; no
mountain is too big to climb if you do it
at your own pace.

What's the best thing to do? That's simple:
            Do your best.
And everything else will fall into place.

—Collin McCarty

Difficult Times in Life
Can Help Us Grow

There are times when we can't explain
the difficulties we face,
but one thing is certain:
we all face them at some point.
There are some difficulties
that shape us for a lifetime,
and some that leave us
only momentarily changed.

Some of us will search
deep within our souls for answers
we may or may not find.
But in that searching,
we may find that
the difficulties we face
will diminish,
and we can come to accept
not only what we've come through,
but the pain we've experienced,
as well.

—Sherrie L. Householder

Sometimes, It's Best to Let Something Go and Begin Again

Things happen in our lives
that we find hard to accept.
Thoughts come back to trouble us
time and time again.
When something happens in our lives
that we find difficult to accept,
we must decide if there is anything
we can do to change things.
If there is, we must do
what we can to make things right again.
But if we have done all we can,
and we know in our hearts that there
is nothing more we can do about it now,
then we should let go of
whatever is troubling us.

After going over all the
"what ifs" and "whys,"
we may learn a valuable lesson.
And we find that even though
it was painful,
we grew through the experience.
Just learning to let things go,
rather than worrying about
what might have been,
might eventually be worth even more
than whatever it is we had to let go of.

—Barbara Cage

You Can Overcome
Any Problems That Life Has to Offer

I know that lately you
have been having problems
and I just want you to know
that you can rely on me
  for anything
you might need
But more important
keep in mind at all times
that you are very capable
of dealing with any complications
that life has to offer
So
do whatever you must
feel whatever you must
and keep in mind at all times
that we all
grow wiser and
become more sensitive and
are able to enjoy life more
after we go through
hard times

—Susan Polis Schutz

Hard Times Can Help Us
Appreciate Life Even More

Sometimes, we all have to feel
alone and frightened before
we can appreciate the life
that surrounds us.
Life changes as we grow,
and we must learn to accept this.
The more we learn, the more we grow.
Hurting, being scared,
feeling alone, and crying
are part of the learning process;
understanding our feelings
makes life challenging
and rewarding.
Going through difficult times
makes you who you are.

You have taken one of
the most significant steps
you will ever have to.
Enter each new day
telling yourself that
you deserve to smile.
Enter each new day believing
that you can make
someone else smile inside,
because you are a beautiful person.
Your kind of beauty is inside you,
and it fills the world
with your presence.
People can feel that.
Be happy; your whole life
  is ahead of you.
It is your life, your chance
to be who and what you want to be.

—Traci Sinclair-Dyer

The Best Way to Make It Through...
Is to Listen to Your Heart

In life, we have to
  make decisions
that aren't easy.
We're afraid that
  whatever choice we make
will upset someone we love.
It is at these times
that we need to look inside
and listen to
  the voice that's inside us.
If we listen just to
  the wishes of those around us
and ignore our own feelings,
we will not be truly happy.
Listen to what you know
  is right
and stand on that,
because when you do,
you will be happy.

—Bethanie Jean Brevik

Always Have Faith in Yourself

It is not easy to
   live life sometimes
and face the world with a smile
when you're crying inside.
It takes a lot of courage
to reach down inside yourself,
hold on to that strength
   that's still there,
and know that tomorrow
is a new day —
   with new possibilities.

But if you can just hold on
long enough to see this through,
you'll come out a new person —
   stronger,
with more understanding,
and with a new pride in yourself
   from knowing you made it.

—Kathy Obara

Everything will be fine...
you'll see

We do what we can.
And we do it with what we've got
   inside of us.

Even if you may forget it sometimes,
I'm here to remind you
that you are a very special person.

I have so much faith in you.
And I know that you'll be able to
do the things you want and need to do.

And if you ever — ever — need me...

   I'll be here for you.

—Carey Martin

With Understanding and Patience, You Can Find a Way Through Any Difficulty

The pressures that life brings each of us can often be too great to deal with, and in turn can make us lose our self-perspective. Eventually, we start seeing everything in a negative light — including ourselves. We may become trapped within ourselves, and without the ability to think clearly, we may choose a way out that causes even more confusion. But don't feel alone, because this has happened to everyone at one time.
Sometimes, life is not meant to be easy; we have to work hard to get what we want so it will be appreciated more when we get it.

Opportunities do not always come
searching for us; we must put in time
and effort to look for them, and even
more to finally achieve them.
It will take time before all the
pieces fit together, but you must be
patient and allow yourself all the
time you need to work things out.
Do not ever give up or give in,
because there is always a way.
Just learn to trust yourself to choose
the right way, and if it shouldn't
work out, try again. Keep trying
until you get it right, and in the
meantime, be patient.
And when it is over, there will be a
reward — not of materialistic value,
but of self-value, which is
accomplishment, inner peace, and
self-growth. This is a valuable
reward that can only be obtained by the
learning experiences that each of us
must face in our own time.

—Dottie Sarisky

Have Confidence
in Your Abilities

Within you is a spirit
capable of touching the stars.
Within you is the ability
to achieve your goals
and make your dreams come true.
Don't listen to others
or fear competition
or worry about wrong choices.
In every experience
there is wisdom
to be gained.
Have faith in yourself
and move ahead with confidence,
believing that you will fulfill
your potential
as the unique person
you were created to be.

—Mary Hough Foote

Until Things Are
Going Your Way Again . . .

Things have not been
going your way lately.
I wish I could make it better
with a hug and a smile,
but unfortunately,
I know that is just not enough.

I know that sometimes it seems
as though everything is against you,
but it is at those times
you must realize
that I am always with you.

Things soon will turn around for you,
and all of this will be
just a small setback
on your path to success.
Until that time comes,
remember that I am here for you
with a hug, a smile,
and a willingness to help you
in any way I can.

— Cindy-Lee Emery

Always Remember
the Strength Within You

Tomorrow might seem
as if it will never come
when your difficulties
continue to absorb
all of your efforts.
But there is hope
that a better tomorrow is near;
there is strength within you
that will help you bear
all the burdens of today.

—jodi mae

Be Easy on Yourself

Our days can sometimes be
  very confusing.
We seem to have too many things to do,
too many problems to solve,
and not enough time to accomplish
  everything.
We tend to forget that each day
is a beautiful miracle,
and there is much love and enjoyment
to be experienced.
You don't have to solve every problem
or accomplish all your goals in one day.
Finish what you can today,
and leave the rest for tomorrow.

Allow yourself time to relax,
time to be with your friends and
  loved ones,
time to play,
and time to sit in the sunshine.
Be easy on yourself,
and you will find your problems
are easier to solve
and that you can accomplish more
with your time.
And you will also find
that your life is more peaceful,
your days are more fun,
and that you are happier
and more content.

—Donna Levine

Tomorrow Is a New Day

Sometimes we do not feel
  like we want to feel
Sometimes we do not achieve
  what we want to achieve
Sometimes things that happen
  do not make sense
Sometimes life leads us in directions
   that are
beyond our control
It is at these times, most of all
that we need someone
who will quietly understand us
and be there to support us
I want you to know
that I am here for you
in every way
and remember that though
things may be difficult now
tomorrow is a new day

—Susan Polis Schutz

For You, Whenever
You're Feeling Alone

We all have those moments when
things aren't quite right . . .
and when the best medicine of all
would just be to know
that there's someone out there
who really cares . . .
and who really values you
for being the wonderful person
you truly are.

Someone does care.
And that someone is me.

And if you ever have a bad day
or a period of time when everything
seems to be going wrong,
and you wonder if anything
could make it right again . . .
      remember . . .

You never have to feel alone.
When you think of who cares . . .
   think of me.
Remember me, or call me
  on the phone and give me
    a chance to remind you
        how special you are to me.
Because you are.
And you always will be.

                              —Alin Austin

Look to the Future
and Brighter Days Ahead

Sometimes it seems like the world
is crumbling around us
   and we just can't go on.
But those are the times when
we most need to look to the future,
to hold on to our faith and hope
   and to each other.

One of the hardest things to accept
is the realization that
   things that make no sense
      to us now
may never make any sense,
but life will go on anyway —
with no explanations or apologies,
and that we somehow survive
the changes thrust upon us.

We even manage to grow. . .
but nothing grows without rain,
so when it begins to pour,
   let it flow.
And when the storm has passed,
   let it go.
Be kind to yourself;
ask for what you need.
   You are not alone.

—Kerry McCaskill

Always Hope for the Best

Don't let go of hope.
Hope gives you the strength
to keep going
when you feel like giving up.
Don't ever quit believing in yourself.
As long as you believe you can,
you will have a reason for trying.
Don't let anyone hold your happiness
in their hands;
hold it in yours,
so it will always be within your reach.
Don't measure success or failure
by material wealth,
but by how you feel;
our feelings determine
the richness of our lives.
Don't let bad moments overcome you;
be patient, and they will pass.

Don't hesitate to reach out for help;
we all need it from time to time.
Don't run away from love
  but towards love,
because it is our deepest joy.
Don't wait for what you want
to come to you.
Go after it with all that you are,
knowing that life will meet you halfway.
Don't feel like you've lost
when plans and dreams fall short
  of your hopes.
Anytime you learn something new
about yourself or about life,
you have progressed.
Don't do anything that takes away
from your self-respect.
Feeling good about yourself
is essential to feeling good about life.
Don't ever forget how to laugh
or be too proud to cry.
It is by doing both
that we live life to its fullest.

—Nancye Sims

No Matter What,
Have Confidence in Yourself

The most difficult thing at times
is to find enough strength
to believe in yourself.

Don't be surprised every now and then
to find yourself with no one
  other than yourself
to defend your beliefs.
The most difficult time
to have faith in your abilities
is when you are the only one,
but that doesn't make
your potential any less,
or decrease your desire
to achieve everything you want.

You have been blessed
  with so many gifts;
all that is needed
is that you find the courage
to continue doing
whatever you believe in.

—Lee Wheeler

Your Dreams Can Come True If . . .

Dreams can come true
if you take the time to
think about what you want in life . . .
Get to know yourself
Find out who you are
Choose your goals carefully
Be honest with yourself
But don't think about yourself so much
that you analyze every word and action
Don't become preoccupied with yourself
Find many interests and pursue them
Find out what is important to you
Find out what you are good at
Don't be afraid to make mistakes
Work hard to achieve successes
When things are not going right
don't give up — just try harder
Find courage inside of you to remain strong

Give yourself freedom to try out new things
Don't be so set in your ways that you can't grow
Always act in an ethical way
Laugh and have a good time
Form relationships with people you respect
Treat others as you want them to treat you
Be honest with people
Accept the truth
Speak the truth
Open yourself up to love
Don't be afraid to love
Remain close to your family
Take part in the beauty of nature
Be appreciative of all that you have
Help those less fortunate than you
Try to make other lives happy
Work towards peace in the world
Live life to the fullest

Dreams can come true
and I hope that all your dreams
become a reality

—Susan Polis Schutz

Life's Disappointments
Always Lead to
Better Tomorrows

In life,
though there may be pain
and sorrow,
along the way also lies
a great happiness.
Though your world feels broken,
pick up what's good
and move on,
for somehow your desires
will find fulfillment.

Remember that
in the end, the ups and downs
will balance themselves.
Cry your tears,
smile your smiles,
but never, never surrender.
Remember that
in yourself lies the strength
to believe that your dreams
are always close by,
even when they seem to be
farthest away.

—Linda Principe

You Can Do It

Look within.
And listen to your heart.
You can do it.
You can reach that goal.
You can make that new reality
  instead of accepting things
    the way they used to be.

You can do it.
All of your highest hopes are
  with you.
Nothing will hold you back but
  your own fears.

And if those fears were created
  by you, they can be
    dealt with by you . . .
      and said good-bye to.

You can do it.
Say it to yourself, and believe it
  in your heart.
Make every single day
  a positive start
    leading to a better and
      bright tomorrow.

      You can do it.

      You really can.

—Alin Austin

Always Believe in Yourself
and in Your Dreams

In the pursuit of any dream,
there will be moments
when it seems that
the dream is lost.
It is then that you must have faith
in the person that you are.
Believe that you have
the ability to overcome
any obstacle standing in your way,
and when your dream comes true,
you will realize then
what a stronger person
you have become.

—Lynn Brown

Live One Day at a Time

We cannot change the past;
we just need to keep
the good memories
and acquire wisdom
from the mistakes we've made.
We cannot predict the future;
we just need to hope and pray
for the best and what is right,
and believe that's how it will be.
We can live a day at a time,
enjoying the present
and always seeking to become
a more loving and better person.

— Karen Berry

Things might look a little cloudy now,
but they'll get better soon.
Just remember that it's true:
    it takes rain to make rainbows,
    lemons to make lemonade,
    and sometimes it takes difficulties
    to make us stronger and better people.

The sun will shine again soon . . . you'll see.

—Collin McCarty

ACKNOWLEDGMENTS

We gratefully acknowledge the permission granted by the following authors to reprint their works.

Sherrie L. Householder for "From Every Change in Life..." and "Difficult Times in Life Can Help Us Grow." Copyright © Sherrie L. Householder, 1990. All rights reserved. Reprinted by permission.

Barbara Cage for "Sometimes, It's Best to Let Something Go . . . ." Copyright © Barbara Cage, 1990. All rights reserved. Reprinted by permission.

Traci Sinclair-Dyer for "Hard Times Can Help Us Appreciate Life Even More." Copyright © Traci Sinclair-Dyer, 1990. All rights reserved. Reprinted by permission.

Bethanie Jean Brevik for "The Best Way to Make It Through . . . ." Copyright © Bethanie Jean Brevik, 1990. All rights reserved. Reprinted by permission.

Kathy Obara for "Always Have Faith in Yourself." Copyright © Kathy Obara, 1990. All rights reserved. Reprinted by permission.

Dottie Sarisky for "With Understanding and Patience . . . ." Copyright © Dottie Sarisky, 1990. All rights reserved. Reprinted by permission.

Mary Hough Foote for "Have Confidence in Your Abilities." Copyright © Mary Hough Foote, 1990. All rights reserved. Reprinted by permission.

Cindy-Lee Emery for "Until Things Are Going Your Way Again . . . ." Copyright © Cindy-Lee Emery, 1990. All rights reserved. Reprinted by permission.

jodi mae for "Always Remember the Strength Within You." Copyright © jodi mae, 1990. All rights reserved. Reprinted by permission.

Donna Levine for "Be Easy on Yourself." Copyright © Donna Levine, 1990. All rights reserved. Reprinted by permission.

Kerry McCaskill for "Look to the Future and Brighter Days Ahead." Copyright © Kerry McCaskill, 1990. All rights reserved. Reprinted by permission.

Lee Wheeler for "No Matter What, Have Confidence in Yourself." Copyright © Lee Wheeler, 1990. All rights reserved. Reprinted by permission.

Linda Principe for "Life's Disappointments Always Lead to Better Tomorrows." Copyright © Linda Principe, 1990. All rights reserved. Reprinted by permission.

A careful effort has been made to trace the ownership of poems used in this anthology in order to obtain permission to reprint copyrighted materials and to give proper credit to the copyright owners.

If any error or omission has occurred, it is completely inadvertent, and we would like to make corrections in future editions provided that written notification is made to the publisher: BLUE MOUNTAIN PRESS, INC., P.O. BOX 4549, Boulder, Colorado 80306.